ADVANTAGE Test Prep 2

MW00830504

Table of Contents

Table of Contents

Math

Practice Test

CREDITS

Concept Development: Kent Publishing Services, Inc.

Written by: Michael Silverstone

Editor: Carla Hamaguchi

Designer: Moonhee Pak

Illustrator: Darcy Tom

Art Director: Tom Cochrane

Project Director: Carolea Williams

Introduction

Testing is a big part of education today, and this workbook is designed to help students become better prepared to succeed at taking standardized and proficiency tests. This workbook contains skills and strategies that can be used in any kind of testing situation. Even if students don't have to take standardized tests, they will still benefit from studying the skills and strategies in this workbook.

Standardized Tests

Standardized tests get their name because they are administered in the exact same way to hundreds of thousands of students across the country. They are also referred to as *norm-referenced tests*. Norms give educators a common standard of measurement of students' skills and abilities across the country. Students are ranked according to their test scores and then assigned a percentile ranking. This ranking tells what percent of all students scored better or worse than the norm.

Proficiency Tests

Many states develop their own statewide proficiency tests. Proficiency tests are also known as *criterion-referenced tests*. This means that the test is based on a list of standards and skills (criteria). States develop standards for what students should know at each grade level. The proficiency test evaluates how well students have mastered these standards.

Although both tests may look similar, they measure different things. A proficiency test measures a student's mastery of set standards. A standardized test compares a student's achievement to others who took the same test across the country.

Many tests were reviewed in developing the material for this workbook. They include the following:
- **California Achievement Tests (CAT)**
- **Comprehensive Tests of Basic Skills (CTBS)**
- **TerraNova**
- **Iowa Tests of Basic Skills (ITBS)**
- **Metropolitan Achievement Tests (MAT)**
- **Stanford Achievement Tests (SAT)**
- **Texas Assessment of Knowledge and Skills (TAKS)**

It is important to recognize that all national standardized achievement tests work essentially the same way. They ask multiple-choice questions, have specific time limits, and compare your child's results to national averages. The goal of this test-prep series is to teach **test-taking strategies** so that no matter which test your child is required to take, he or she will be successful.

Introduction

Preparing for Tests

The more students are prepared for taking standardized and proficiency tests, the better they will do on those tests. A student who understands the skills commonly measured and who practices test-taking strategies will be more likely to be a successful test-taker. The more the student knows and knows what to expect, the more comfortable he or she will be in actual test-taking situations.

Standardized and proficiency testing is used to:

- evaluate students' progress, strengths, and weaknesses.
- show how each student's school achievement compares with other students on a local and nationwide level (standardized).
- show an individual student's achievement of set standards (proficiency).
- select students for remedial or achievement programs.
- tell educators whether school systems are succeeding.
- evaluate the success of school programs.
- help educators develop programs to suit their students' specific needs.

Standardized tests are only one measure of student achievement, however. Teachers use many other methods to gain insights into each student's skills, abilities, and knowledge. They evaluate students through day-to-day observation, evaluation, and assessment.

Introduction

How Can Parents Help Children Succeed at Standardized Testing?

The following list includes suggestions on how to help prepare children to do their best on standardized tests:

Tips for Parents

- Monitor your child's progress.

- Get to know your child's teacher; find out what he or she thinks you can do to best help your child at home.

- Be informed about your state's testing requirements.

- Motivate your child to prepare.

- Help your child structure a quiet place and time away from distractions to do homework.

- Read aloud to your child.

- Find learning experiences in everyday life, making change, reading signs, preparing food, walking outside.

- Make sure your child is getting the sleep and nutrition he or she needs to succeed.

- Always nurture your child's curiosity and desire to learn.

- Encourage your child to learn about computers and technology.

- Encourage your child to take tests seriously, but to value learning and giving one's best efforts.

- Notice academic efforts your child is making and support and acknowledge what you see.

Where Can I Learn More About Testing?

ERIC Clearinghouse on Assessment and Evaluation
209 O'Boyle Hall
The Catholic University of America
Washington, DC 20064
(202) 319-5120
http://ericae.net/

National Center for Fair and Open Testing, Inc. (FairTest)
342 Broadway
Cambridge, MA 02139
http://www.fairtest.org/

Introduction to Reading

Reading is an important part of life and one of the most vital skills required for success on standardized and proficiency tests as well as in many careers. The best way for children to improve reading skills is to become avid readers. The most successful readers read for pleasure. They tend to read often, with others and alone. They read many different types of materials as a natural habit. The more children read, the more fluent they become. This tends to make reading more rewarding. Research has found a direct connection between the amount of time a child reads and high academic performance as measured on tests.

Nearly every standardized or proficiency test includes a section on reading. The reading passages may be fiction, nonfiction, or poetry. They may also be graphic information like maps or reference information like library catalog cards and dictionaries. Students are asked to recall, interpret, and reflect on what they read.

The following pages give a review of reading skills. They allow students to practice the skills with questions just like the ones they will be expected to answer on tests. In this workbook section, students will prepare for questions that ask them to:

- find words in **context.**

- find **root words.**

- make **predictions.**

- recognize the **beginning, middle, and end** of a narrative.

- **summarize** a passage.

- **draw conclusions** from what an author has written.

- find the connection between **cause and effect.**

- recognize details that **compare or contrast.**

- **ask questions** about a reading selection.

- practice **locating information** in a reading selection.

- **extend meaning** by making connections with a text.

- understand **graphic information** such as maps, charts, graphs, and diagrams.

- use **reference skills** such as alphabetization and use of libraries, dictionaries, and encyclopedias.

Advantage Test Prep Grade 2 © 2004 Creative Teaching Press

The Life of a Seed

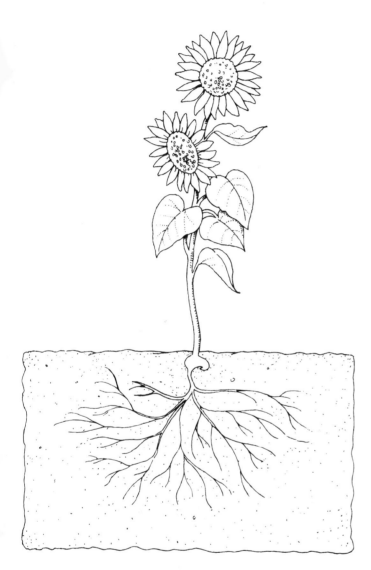

Look at a bowl of dried beans. Do they look alive? Do they seem like something that could grow and change?

Before a seed starts to grow, it is *dormant.* This means it is sleeping. It is not yet a living thing, but it could "wake up" and become living.

To come alive, seeds need certain conditions. They need warmth, water, light, and food. If seeds are frozen, they can't grow. This is why plants stop growing in the winter in cold places.

Water can come from rain or it can come from a watering can. Too much water keeps some seeds from growing.

Plants also need light to grow. Light helps plants make their own food.

Plants also take in food and minerals from soil. Most seeds can sprout without being in soil. They use the food that is inside the seed. There is usually enough food inside a seed to help it grow big enough to become a baby plant.

A sprouted seed sends out roots. These roots can draw food out of soil. At about the same time, the seeds begin to grow the stems and leaves of the plant. As this happens, the baby plant starts its life, growing and reaching toward the light.

Vocabulary

Reading

KNOW THE SKILL: **Words in Context**

Some test questions ask you to figure out the meaning of a word. Often you can guess the meaning of the word by thinking about the meanings of other words around it.

Test Example

1 Before a seed starts to grow, it is <u>dormant</u>.

Which word means the same as *dormant*?

- ○ tall
- ○ leafy
- ○ sleeping

Think About the Answer

The answer is *sleeping*. It can't be *tall* because the seed hasn't started to grow yet. It can't be *leafy* because a seed doesn't have leaves. *Sleeping* makes the most sense.

Now You Try It

2 Choose the word that means the same thing as the underlined word.

Light helps plants make their own food. Plants also take in <u>minerals</u> from the soil.

- ○ light
- ○ food
- ○ water

Check your answer on page 107.

Vocabulary

KNOW THE SKILL: **Root Words**

When you see similar words, decide if they have a common root word. Think about the beginning and ending of the word and how they change the meaning of the root word.

Test Example

 1 Which word describes the picture?

- ○ healthy
- ○ unhealthy
- ○ healthier

Think About the Answer

The answer is *unhealthy*. The picture shows a sick plant. The root word that is in all four choices is *health*. The beginning *un* means "not." *Unhealthy* is another way to say "not healthy."

Now You Try It

 2 Which word describes the picture?

- ○ frozen
- ○ unfrozen
- ○ freezer

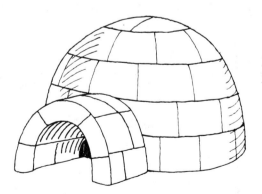

Check your answer on page 107.

Comprehension

KNOW THE SKILL: **Making Predictions**

Predicting is a skill you use every day. Predicting involves recognizing patterns. Your knowledge of patterns helps you know what will happen in the future.

Test Example

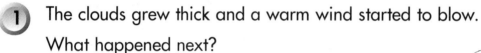

1 The clouds grew thick and a warm wind started to blow.

What happened next?

○   ○   ○

Think About the Answer

The third choice is the best one. The sentence tells you that it got cloudy and windy. The next step is probably rain. The sky in the first choice is too clear. The second choice shows weather that is too cold. The sentence says it was a *warm* wind.

Now You Try It

2 Johnny planted the bean seed in moist soil.

What happened next?

○   ○   ○

Check your answer on page 107.

Advantage Test Prep Grade 2 © 2004 Creative Teaching Press

KNOW THE SKILL: **Time Order Clues**

Use time order words like *before*, *after*, *since*, and *finally* to understand when something happened in the order of events.

Test Example

1 Which word in the sentence is a time order word?

First the baby plants begin to grow leaves so they can take in light.

- ○ first
- ○ leaves
- ○ take

Think About the Answer

The word *first* is a word that we use to say when something happened in time. The other choices are not.

Now You Try It

2 Circle the time order word in this sentence.

A seed sends out roots after it sprouts.

Check your answer on page 107.

Comprehension

Reading

KNOW THE SKILL: **Summarizing**

When you summarize, you tell what is most important. Test questions may ask you to choose a word or a few words that summarize something. Base your choice on what is most important in what you just read.

Test Example

1 What is this sentence about?

The seeds need to be damp.

- ○ seeds
- ○ water
- ○ dampness

Think About the Answer

The sentence is about *seeds*. *Seeds* is the subject of the sentence. *Damp* describes the seeds.

Now You Try It

2 What are these sentences about?

The main source of light for plants is the sun. Plants can grow indoors, but they still need light.

- ○ seeds
- ○ sun
- ○ light

Check your answer on page 107.

Advantage Test Prep Grade 2 © 2004 Creative Teaching Press

The Case of the Missing Card Collection

Joey liked hockey. He had cards of all his favorite players. He liked to collect cards even more than he liked to play hockey. He kept his cards in a big notebook with clear pages.

One day he brought his card collection to school for sharing. He asked Ms. Perez where he should keep it. "Put it on my desk," she said. "It should be safe there."

Finally, it was time for Joey to share. He took the notebook from his teacher's desk. Then he stood before the class. When he opened the notebook, he got a surprise. There were no cards inside, just pages of math problems!

It was a mystery. Where were the cards? Omar raised his hand. He had an idea. Maybe Ms. Willis, who works with math study groups, took Joey's notebook by mistake. Her notebook looked just like his from the outside.

Omar was right. Just then, Ms. Willis came into the room looking for her notebook. She was smiling. She had started teaching her math study group and looked in her notebook to find pages of hockey cards!

Comprehension

KNOW THE SKILL: **Main Idea**

In a main idea question, you will look at a list of different ideas that were in the story. Then you will need to make a choice about which idea is the main idea, or the most important point of the story.

Test Example

1 *Jack and the Beanstalk* is about _____.

- ○ magic beans
- ○ Jack's adventures
- ○ Goldilocks

Think About the Answer

Magic beans are not the most important part of the story. *Goldilocks* is not in the story. The best answer is *Jack's adventures.*

Now You Try It

2 *The Case of the Missing Card Collection* is about _____.

- ○ Ms. Willis' math group
- ○ playing hockey
- ○ when Joey's cards were missing

Check your answer on page 107.

   Advantage Test Prep Grade 2 © 2004 Creative Teaching Press

KNOW THE SKILL: **Drawing Conclusions**

Drawing conclusions is what you do after you read. Look for clues that may tell you what happened before or what could happen next.

Test Example

 1 What happened?

- ○ The wind blew the pot off the ledge.
- ○ A cat knocked the pot to the ground.
- ○ The plant was too heavy.

Think About the Answer

There is a strong wind blowing the curtains. The wind probably blew it off the ledge. A cat is not in the picture. There is nothing in the picture that says the plant was too heavy.

Now You Try It

 2 Why did Ms. Willis take Joey's card collection?

- ○ She wanted it for herself.
- ○ She mistook his notebook for hers.
- ○ She was playing a joke on him.

Check your answer on page 107.

Comprehension

Reading

KNOW THE SKILL: **Cause and Effect**

Cause and effect is the skill of being able to answer the question "Why?" about things that happen. The answer to a cause and effect question usually starts with "because."

Test Example

1 Why is the girl smiling?

○ She just heard a good joke.

○ She got a gift from a friend.

○ She is afraid of dogs.

Think About the Answer

You can see that she is getting a gift. That is the best answer. There is no dog in the drawing. It is possible she heard a good joke, but it is hard to be sure.

Now You Try It

2 Why would Ms. Willis mistake Joey's notebook for hers?

○ They looked alike.

○ Teachers are careless.

○ She needed glasses.

Check your answer on page 107.

Comprehension

KNOW THE SKILL: **Compare and Contrast**

When you compare and contrast, you figure out how things are alike and how they are different. Test questions ask how the meanings of words, events, or characters in a story are alike and different.

Test Example

 1 How are these three things alike?

○ Every one is made from bricks.

○ Each is a place where people live.

○ They all have two floors.

Think About the Answer

One house is made of wood and another is made of ice, so the first answer can't be true. The igloo has only one floor. The second statement is true; each is a place where people live.

Now You Try It

 2 Choose the phrase that best completes the sentence.

In *The Case of the Missing Card Collection*, Joey's notebook was different from Ms. Willis' because _____.

○ it was black

○ the notebook had hockey cards

○ he put it on Ms. Perez' desk

Check your answer on page 107.

Read the poem, "Hopping Frog." Then complete the lessons on pages 19 through 21.

Hopping Frog

by Christina Rossetti

Hopping frog, hop here and be seen,

I'll not pelt you with stick or stone:

Your cap is laced and your coat is green;

Good bye, we'll let each other alone.

Plodding toad, plod here and be looked at,

You the finger of scorn is crooked at:

But though you're lumpish, you're harmless too;

You won't hurt me, and I won't hurt you.

KNOW THE SKILL: **Asking Questions**

Ask yourself questions when you read a poem. A good question will make you think about the important ideas or feelings in the poem.

Test Example

1 Which question would be the best one to ask a new classmate?

○ What do you like to do for fun?

○ How tall are you?

○ What time is it?

Think about the Answer

You can see how tall the person is without having to ask. A clock can tell you what time it is. The first choice is the best, because it could help you learn about a connection between what the new classmate likes to do and what you like.

Now You Try It

2 What does the person in the poem want to know about the frog?

_____

_____

Check your answer on page 107.

KNOW THE SKILL: **Locating Information**

You may not remember everything you read, but you can practice looking back to find out something you have forgotten. To locate information, let your eyes skim over what you have read. Look for the word or words that match what you are looking for.

Test Example

1. What time does recess start?

   ○ 8:50

   ○ 11:20

   ○ 1:25

Class Schedule	
Quiet Start	8:30
Morning Meeting	8:50
Reading Related	9:20
Recess	11:20
Lunch	11:50
Math	12:25
Art	1:25
Science	2:05
Closing Circle	2:55
Dismissal	3:05

Think About the Answer

The correct answer is 11:20. There is no need to read the whole schedule. Just look for the word *recess* and find the time next to it.

Now You Try It

2. The poem says, "Your cap is laced and your coat is green."

   What is green?

   ○ leaves

   ○ pond water

   ○ the frog's coat

Check your answer on page 107.

KNOW THE SKILL: **Extend Meaning**

Try to connect what you have read to what you think, feel, and know. On a test, try out different answers in your mind. See if they seem true to you.

Test Example

1. In the poem "Hopping Frog," the poet thinks we should act _____ toward frogs.

   ○ kind

   ○ mean

   ○ rude

Think About the Answer

The correct answer is *kind.* The poet says that she won't pelt the frog with a stick or stone. She won't hurt him. The poet says the frog is harmless, so there is no reason to be mean or rude to him.

Now You Try It

2. How do you think the poet would act toward a turtle?

   ○ mean

   ○ rude

   ○ gentle

Check your answer on page 107.

KNOW THE SKILL: Map Reading

Some tests will ask you questions about a map. Read the title that tells what the map shows. Look for arrows that show the directions. *N* stands for "North"; *S* stands for "South"; *W* stands for "West"; and *E* stands for "East."

Test Example

1   What is this a map of?

    ○ the United States

    ○ the world

    ○ North America

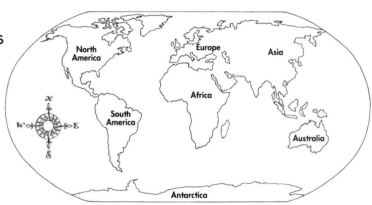

Think about the Answer

The best answer is *the world* because the map shows more than just the United States or North America.

Now You Try It

2   Find Asia on the map. From Asia, which direction is Australia?

    ○ east

    ○ west

    ○ south

Check your answer on page 107.

Graphic Information

KNOW THE SKILL: **Charts and Graphs**

Charts and graphs can help you to "see" numbers in picture form. Read the title and any other information at the bottom or along the side of the chart.

Test Example

1 How many teeth did Ms. Owen's class lose in November?

○ 4 teeth

○ 7 teeth

○ 3 teeth

	Sept.	Oct.	Nov.	Dec.	Jan.	Feb.	Mar.	Apr.	May	June
Tooth Chart for Ms. Owen's Class										
10										
9										
8										
7			x							
6		x	x							
5		x	x						x	
4		x	x	x					x	
3		x	x	x				x	x	
2		x	x	x	x			x	x	x
1		x	x	x	x	x		x	x	x

Think About the Answer

There are four *x*'s above the column for November. The correct answer is *4 teeth*. Notice that *Nov.* is the abbreviation for *November*.

Now You Try It

2 In which month did Ms. Owen's class lose the most teeth?

_____

Check your answer on page 107.

KNOW THE SKILL: **Diagrams**

A diagram is a picture with labels that helps you see the parts of something.

Test Example

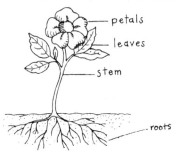

1 What part of a flower is at the very top?

○ petals

○ stem

○ leaves

Flower

petals

leaves

stem

roots

Think About the Answer

Petals are the labeled parts that are at the top of the drawing. The other choices are parts of a flower, but they are not at the top.

Now You Try It

2 Make a labeled diagram of a person in the box. Give your diagram a title. Make sure to show these parts: arms, legs, eyes, ears, nose.

Check your answer on page 107.

Graphic Information

KNOW THE SKILL: **Graphic Organizers**

A graphic organizer uses words and shapes to show how ideas are connected.

Test Example

1 Which of these words belongs in this graphic organizer?

○ blue jays

○ frogs

○ horses

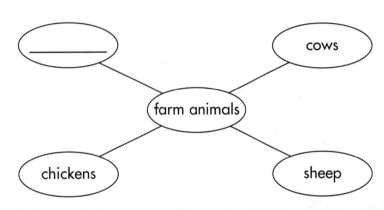

Think About the Answer

The oval in the center says that the main idea of this organizer is farm animals. Blue jays and frogs are animals, but they are not farm animals. *Horses* is the best choice.

Now You Try It

2 What is another word you could add to the graphic organizer?

_____

Check your answer on page 107.

Reference Sources

KNOW THE SKILL: **Alphabet Skills**

To find a word in a dictionary or a subject or name in an index, you need to know ABC order.

Test Example

 Which word comes first in a dictionary?

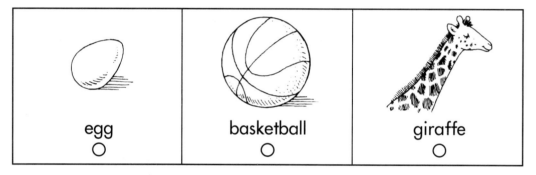

egg ○

basketball ○

giraffe ○

Think About the Answer

The *e* in *egg* comes after the *b* in *basketball*. The *g* in *giraffe* comes even later. *Basketball* would come first in a dictionary.

Now You Try It

 Which word comes first in a dictionary?

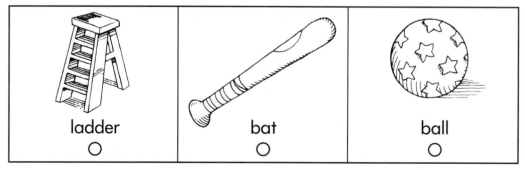

ladder ○

bat ○

ball ○

Check your answer on page 108.

Advantage Test Prep Grade 2 © 2004 Creative Teaching Press

Reference Sources

KNOW THE SKILL: Dictionaries

A dictionary is a book of words that tells what words mean and how to pronounce them. It can also help you find the correct way to spell words.

Test Example

1 Read this definition.

> **engine** (en´ • jən) a machine that makes power to do work.

Where would you find an *engine*?

- ○ inside a flower
- ○ in a car
- ○ under a rock

Think About the Answer

A flower is a living thing, not a *machine*. Machines are not under most rocks. A car is a machine. It has an engine. *In a car* is the best answer.

Now You Try It

2 Read this definition.

> jovial (jō • vē • əl) happy, friendly.

Why might someone feel *jovial*?

- ○ no friends were in sight
- ○ a dog bit the person
- ○ the person won a prize

Check your answer on page 108.

KNOW THE SKILL: **Using a Library**

Library skills are important. It is important to know the difference between fiction, nonfiction, and reference. It is also helpful to know how to use the library catalog system.

Test Example

1 Which of these would be a made-up story?

○ *My First Trip to Jupiter*

○ *The True Book of the Solar System*

○ *A Journey to the Planets*

Topic: Planets

Adams, Chris	*The True Book of the Solar System* (nonfiction)
Bardini, Frank	*Flying to the Moon & Other Poems* (poems)
Science Unlimited	*Our Solar System* (video)
Fernandez, Carlos	*A Journey to the Planets* (nonfiction)
Silvers, Louie	*My First Trip to Jupiter* (fiction)
Thomas, Fred	*Stars and Planets* (nonfiction)

Think About the Answer

My First Trip to Jupiter is the correct answer. It is fiction. That means it is a made-up story. *The True Book of the Solar System* and *A Journey to the Planets* are listed as nonfiction. This means that they have true information.

Now You Try It

2 Which is a book of poems?

○ *Flying to the Moon & Other Poems*

○ *Our Solar System*

○ *Stars and Planets*

Check your answer on page 108.

Advantage Test Prep Grade 2 © 2004 Creative Teaching Press

Reading

KNOW THE SKILL: **Encyclopedia Entries**

An encyclopedia is a book or a set of books that has information on almost every subject. An encyclopedia lists names in ABC order by the letters of their last name.

Test Example

1. In which encyclopedia would you find an entry about Rosa Parks?

   ○ A–B

   ○ R–S

   ○ P–Q

Think About the Answer

Rosa Parks' last name starts with a *p*. *P–Q* is the correct answer.

Now You Try It

2. In which encyclopedia would you find an entry about Alabama?

   ○ A–B

   ○ X–Z

   ○ R–S

Check your answer on page 108.

Understanding Writing Prompts

On many tests, students will be asked to write about something. They will be given time to plan their writing, write, and revise their writing.

The writing section of a test has a special instruction called the **prompt.** It tells students what to write about. Here are some examples of the kinds of prompts that students might see on a writing test:

- Tell about a special day you had with a friend.

- Take a story you know. Write a new chapter for it.

- Pretend you are a character in a story you know. Write a letter to another character.

- Tell about a time you did something that made you feel proud.

- Describe someone you like or love.

- If you could be any animal, which one would you want to be? Give a few reasons why.

- Tell about a book you like. Say why you think it is a good book.

- Who do you look up to? Say why.

- Tell about something you value that doesn't cost money. Explain why it is valuable to you.

Students should read the writing prompt carefully and be sure to understand what it is asking. Here are some general tips for students to think about before they start to write:

- Try to see pictures in your mind and write what you see.

- If you are writing a story, introduce your characters by telling their names and saying what they are like at the beginning of your story.

- Give details that tell what things look like, sound like, smell like, and feel like.

- Think about books you like—it can be helpful to make your stories like the ones in those books.

- After you finish, read over what you wrote and see if you left out any words or ideas that you can add.

- When you think you are done, read over your writing again to check your spelling.

- Make sure sentences start with a capital letter and end with an end mark.

- In your final draft, make sure to form your letters neatly enough that someone else will have no trouble reading what you wrote.

Writing

The box below is called a **rubric.** Rubrics are used to score different parts of writing on a test. The numbers in this rubric have these meanings:

4	Excellent
3	Good
2	Just okay
1	Not good enough
0	Not really finished

Four areas in which your writing can be graded are explained below.

Part of Writing	Description	Score
Ideas	Do you have ideas to share with a reader?	
Organization	Does your writing move from part to part in a way a reader can understand?	
Sentence Structure	Are your sentences complete and easy to understand?	
Spelling, Punctuation, and Grammar	Can you spell second-grade spelling words correctly? Do your sentences start with a capital letter and end with a punctuation mark?	

Your writing will usually get a number grade (4, 3, 2, 1, or 0) in each of these areas. These numbers are added together to give a number score to your writing. When you evaluate your score by category, you will be able to see in which areas you need to improve.

Prewriting

Before you start writing, you may want to choose one of these strategies to help you warm up your brain and organize your ideas. You can use the special area of the test for drawing, writing, and planning before you jump into the writing.

Make a Sketch

For many people, writing starts with a picture they see in their mind. Drawing a quick picture can help writers think and start to describe the picture they see.

This is my dog, Barky. She follows me everywhere.

Story Planner

If you are writing a story, you may want to show the steps of your story in boxes. It can help if you make pictures for the beginning, the middle, and the end. Pictures like this give you a plan you can follow so you don't lose track of the story.

When you are writing about a topic, you can use a mind map to think of different ideas that you could include. Put the name of the topic in a circle in the middle of the map. Draw lines from the middle circle and write other ideas you think of in the circles connected to the lines.

Mind Map

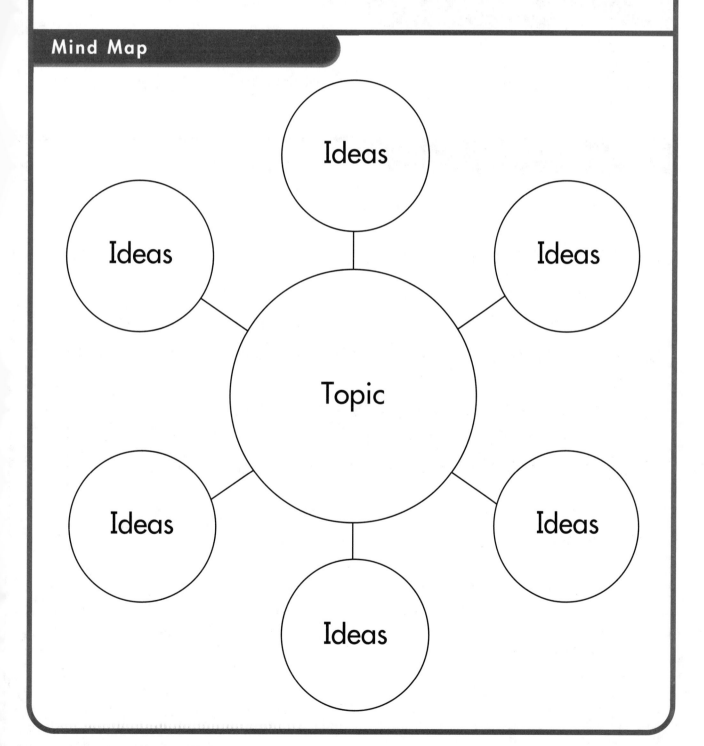

Writing Starters

Read the writing prompt below. Then read the checklist to make sure you have a plan to do your best.

Writing Prompt

Tell about a special day you spent with a friend or family member. Tell what you did on that day and why it was a special time for you. Use details so that the reader can know what you saw, felt, and did on this day.

Writer's Checklist

Check to make sure that you think about each of these points when you write your story:

☐ My story talks about a special day with a friend or family member.

☐ I talk about at least three different things that happened that day.

☐ I made sure to use details to show what the day was like.

☐ My story has an introduction, a middle, and an end that tells why the day was special for me.

☐ I have spelled second-grade spelling words right.

☐ Names and beginnings of sentences start with a capital letter.

☐ My sentences end with a period (.), a question mark (?), or an exclamation point (!).

Advantage Test Prep Grade 2 © 2004 Creative Teaching Press

Plan Your Writing

Use this space to plan your writing. You can use it to make a sketch, a story planner, a mind map, an outline, a list, or whatever will help you start to get your ideas down on paper.

Sketch

Story Planner

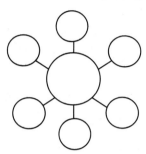

Mind Map

Writing

_____

_____

_____

_____

_____

_____

_____

_____

_____

_____

_____

_____

_____

_____

Use separate sheets of paper if you need more room.

Advantage Test Prep Grade 2 © 2004 Creative Teaching Press

Write Your Final Draft

Before you start your final draft, go back to the checklist on page 34 and use it to review your first draft. You can change things to make your first draft better. Then write your final draft. Use extra sheets of paper if needed.

_____

_____

_____

_____

_____

_____

_____

_____

_____

_____

_____

_____

_____

_____

Give Yourself a Score

Go back to the Writing Rubric on page 31. Give yourself a score from 4 to 0 for each category. Then ask someone else to score your writing so you will have two different sets of scores.

How I Scored It

Ideas	Organization	Sentence Structure	Spelling, Punctuation, and Grammar
_____	_____	_____	_____

How Someone Else Scored It

Ideas	Organization	Sentence Structure	Spelling, Punctuation, and Grammar
_____	_____	_____	_____

Advantage Test Prep Grade 2 © 2004 Creative Teaching Press

There are many different language skills that help us use English well. Some of the skills students can expect to see on a test are spelling, grammar, and punctuation.

One of the best ways to improve language skills is to read. Whenever we read, we learn how language is used. The more we read, the more it becomes part of us.

Here is a list of key skills students will learn and practice in this section:

- Complete Sentences
- End Marks
- Capital Letters
- Contractions
- Commas
- Nouns
- Verbs
- Verb Tenses
- Synonyms
- Antonyms
- Similes
- Connecting Words
- Comparisons: *-er* and *-est*
- Spelling

KNOW THE SKILL: **Complete Sentences**

A sentence is complete when it has a noun and a verb. It must also end with a period, a question mark, or an exclamation point.

Test Example

1 Which of these is a complete sentence?

○ a long time ago.

○ He lived a long time ago.

○ A long time ago he.

Think About the Answer

The answer is *He lived a long time ago.* The action word in this sentence is *lived.* The person in the sentence is *he.* The sentence starts with a capital letter and ends with a period. No other choice follows all these rules.

Now You Try It

2 Jason _____ the ball.

Which word makes this a complete sentence?

○ foot

○ kicked

○ careful

Check your answer on page 108.

KNOW THE SKILL: **End Marks**

Every sentence should have an end mark. A regular sentence that makes a statement ends with a period. A question ends with a question mark. If you have a sentence that makes an exciting statement, it ends with an exclamation point.

Test Example

1. Which end mark is missing?

   Is she seven years old

   ○ ? (question mark)

   ○ . (period)

   ○ ! (exclamation point)

Think About the Answer

The sentence needs a question mark because it is asking for information. The other two marks are used when making a statement or an exciting statement.

Now You Try It

2. Write one question, one statement, and one exclamation.

   Question: _____

   Statement: _____

   Exclamation: _____

Check your answer on page 108.

Language

KNOW THE SKILL: **Capital Letters**

The first word of every sentence should always begin with a capital letter. Other words that begin with capitals include names of specific people and places, days of the week, and months of the year.

Test Example

1 Which sentence is correct?

○ did you brush your teeth?

○ We live in Chicago.

○ You can come with us on saturday.

Think About the Answer

The second sentence is correct. The first sentence is missing a capital letter at the beginning. The last sentence is missing a capital letter at the beginning of *saturday*.

Now You Try It

2 Write a sentence that has a city or state's name in it.

_____

_____

Check your answer on page 108.

Advantage Test Prep Grade 2 © 2004 Creative Teaching Press

Mechanics

KNOW THE SKILL: **Contractions**

Contractions are formed when two words are combined to make one shorter word. An apostrophe (') stands in for the missing letters.

Test Example

1 What two words make up the contraction *we'll*?

○ we well

○ we will

○ will we

Think About the Answer

We will are the words that make up the contraction *we'll*. The apostrophe (') stands in for the dropped letters *wi* from *will*.

Now You Try It

2 Write a contraction for each pair of words.

he + will _____

let + us _____

could + not _____

you + are _____

that + is _____

I + am _____

Check your answer on page 108.

Language

KNOW THE SKILL: **Commas**

Use a comma between the numbers in a date *(July 4, 1776)*. Commas also belong in between the things in a list of three or more items *(red, white, and blue)*.

Test Example

1 Choose the sentence that is correct.

○ I need, a new coat hat and scarf.

○ I need a new coat, hat, and scarf.

○ I need a new coat hat and, scarf.

Think About the Answer

The second choice is correct; it has commas between each item in the list.

Now You Try It

2 Rewrite this sentence correctly by adding commas.

The flag of France is red white and blue.

_____

_____

_____

Check your answer on page 108.

KNOW THE SKILL: **Nouns**

A **noun** is the name of a person, a place, or a thing. Often the noun is the thing that the sentence is about.

Test Example

1 Which is the noun?

LaToya is very smart.

- ○ LaToya
- ○ very
- ○ smart

Think About the Answer

The sentence is about LaToya. LaToya is a person. Her name is the noun in the sentence. The other choices are describing words. They are not nouns. Remember, there is often more than one noun in a sentence.

Now You Try It

2 Write the three nouns from the sentence on the lines.

Laura made eggs for Mom.

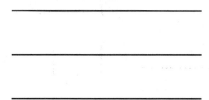

_____

_____

_____

Check your answer on page 108.

Grammar and Usage

KNOW THE SKILL: **Verbs**

Verbs can be action words that describe what is happening. They can also express a "state of being." These "state of being" verbs include: *is, am, are, was, were, am, be,* and *been.*

Test Example

1 Which is the verb in this sentence?

Steve is my younger brother.

○ Steve

○ is

○ younger

Think About the Answer

The "state of being" verb in this sentence is *is. Steve* is a noun, not a verb. The word *younger* is an adjective, a describing word.

Now You Try It

2 Write the verb from the sentence on the line.

She made me a card on my birthday.

_____

Check your answer on page 108.

Language

KNOW THE SKILL: **Verb Tenses**

Verbs that talk about what is happening right now usually end in *ing* or *s*, such as *cleaning* or *cleans*. Verbs that talk about what happened in the past usually end in *ed*, such as *cleaned*.

Test Example

1 Choose the sentence that makes the action happen now.

○ My dog will lick my nose.

○ My dog licked my nose.

○ My dog is licking my nose.

Think About the Answer

The answer is *My dog is licking my nose*. It expresses something happening right now. The first sentence expresses something that is going to happen in the future. The second expresses something that has already happened.

Now You Try It

2 Which verb does NOT belong in the group?

smiling, washing, grows, talking

○ eats

○ listening

○ climbed

Check your answer on page 108.

KNOW THE SKILL: **Synonyms**

Synonyms are two different words with similar meanings. *Hot* and *warm* are synonyms. They are alike because both are about heat.

Test Example

1 What is another word for *happy*?

○ glad

○ shiny

○ silly

Think About the Answer

The closest match is *glad. Shiny* has a much different meaning than *happy. Silly* does not mean the same as *happy.*

Now You Try It

2 Write a different word with the SAME meaning.

small _____   begin _____

pretty _____   end _____

cold _____   job _____

fast _____   large _____

nice _____

Check your answer on page 108.

Grammar and Usage

Language

KNOW THE SKILL: **Antonyms**

Antonyms are two words with opposite meanings. The words *up* and *down* are antonyms. So are the words *good* and *bad.* Antonyms can help you understand ideas.

Test Example

1 The OPPOSITE of *new* is _____.

○ fresh

○ young

○ old

Think About the Answer

Old is the correct answer. *Old* is the opposite of *new. Fresh* is more like *new* than the opposite of *new.* The same is true of *young.*

Now You Try It

2 Write a different word with the OPPOSITE meaning.

giant _____   cold _____

ugly _____   full _____

hot _____   happy _____

wet _____   clean _____

bright _____

Check your answer on page 108.

Language

KNOW THE SKILL: **Similes**

Similes are words that compare one thing to another. A test question about a simile usually uses the word *like* or *as.*

Test Example

1 A rabbit is as fast as _____.
- ○ snow
- ○ lightning
- ○ wood

Think About the Answer

Snow is not known for being fast. *Wood* doesn't really move. *Lightning* streaks across the sky quickly. It is the choice that best completes the simile.

Now You Try It

2 My apple pie is _____ like an oven.
- ○ small
- ○ cold
- ○ hot

Check your answer on page 108.

Advantage Test Prep Grade 2 © 2004 Creative Teaching Press

Language

KNOW THE SKILL: **Connecting Words**

You may be asked to connect a sentence that has two parts. Use *and* to connect equal parts. Use *but* to connect one part that depends on the other part. Use *or* when you want to give a choice about which part is true.

Test Example

1 Which word best completes the sentence?

I will tell you _____ you have to keep it secret.

  ○ and

  ○ but

  ○ or

Think About the Answer

But is the best choice. *And* could be used in this sentence, but it does not show a connection between the two ideas in the sentence as well as *but* does.

Now You Try It

2 Write a connecting word to complete the sentence.

The movie cost a lot of money _____ we did not have much left.

Check your answer on page 108.

Language

KNOW THE SKILL: **Comparisons: -er and -est**

The word endings *-er* and *-est* tell you how things compare. The ending *-er* tells you something is more than another. The ending *-est* tells you that something is the most of all. Here are some examples: *fast, fast**er**, fast**est**; happy, happ**ier**, happ**iest**.*

Test Example

1 Choose the word that fixes the mistake in this sentence.

It was the <u>most pretty</u> butterfly I've ever seen.

- ○ pretty
- ○ prettier
- ● prettiest

Think About the Answer

The sentence is saying that the butterfly is not just pretty and not just prettier than another butterfly. *Prettiest* is the correct answer.

Now You Try It

2 Write the form of *slow* that fits in the sentence.

The snail was __slower__ than the grasshopper.

Check your answer on page 108.

KNOW THE SKILL: **Adding Suffixes**

To spell properly, you need to know how to add -s, -ed, and -ing to words. In most cases, adding -s makes a noun plural, adding -ed makes a verb past tense, and adding -ing makes a verb present tense.

Test Example

1 Choose the word that should take the place of the underlined word.

We <u>plays</u> football yesterday.

- ○ play
- ◉ played
- ○ playing

Think About the Answer

Played is correct. It is the past tense of *play*.

Now You Try It

2 Choose the word that should replace the underlined word.

I am <u>rows</u> a boat with my sister.

- ○ rowed
- ○ row
- ◉ rowing

Check your answer on page 108.

Language

KNOW THE SKILL: **Compound Words**

Many words are compound words. A **compound word** is a word made of two parts. Understanding compound words can help you be a better speller.

Test Example

1 What two words make up the compound word *bathtub*?

_____ + _____

Think About the Answer

When you say the word, you can easily hear each syllable. Listen to the sounds of the word and you will hear that the words *bath* and *tub* make up the compound word *bathtub*.

Now You Try It

2 What two words make up the compound word *racetrack*?

_____ + _____

Check your answer on page 108.

Introduction to Mathematics

Mathematics is a language. You use this language when you buy, measure, cook, build, count and use a calendar. It is important to practically every career. An understanding of mathematics helps students solve problems and comprehend ideas. Most standardized tests have math sections that address a broad range of skills.

By studying this section of the workbook, students will develop math skills and learn how to perform better on tests. Mastering these skills will help students understand and use math on tests and in all that they do.

- Place Value
- Odd and Even Numbers
- Number Order (Before, After, Between)
- Skip Counting by 2, 5, and 10
- Greater Than and Less Than
- Ordinal Numbers
- Solve for a Missing Number
- Fact Families
- Counting Money
- Telling Time
- Measurement
- Estimating
- Addition with 2-Digit Numbers
- Subtraction with 2-Digit Numbers
- Fractions
- Identifying Shapes
- Congruent Shapes
- Symmetry
- Finding Patterns
- Function Boxes
- Showing Data
- Making a Plan
- Showing Your Work

KNOW THE SKILL: **Place Value**

When we read a number like 123, each of the numerals has a different value. The 1 in the hundreds place = 100. The 2 in the tens place = 20. The 3 in the ones place = 3.
100 + 20 + 3 = 123.

Test Example

1 How many blocks are there?

○ 40

○ 34

○ 44

Think About the Answer

The correct answer is 34. There are three rows of 10 blocks.
10 + 10 + 10 = 30. There is one row with four blocks. Altogether, there are 30 + 4 blocks. 30 + 4 = 34.

Now You Try It

2 How many blocks are there?

○ 50

○ 55

○ 65

Check your answer on page 108.

KNOW THE SKILL: **Odd and Even Numbers**

Even numbers can be divided exactly into two equal whole numbers with nothing left over. When you divide an odd number into two, one will be left over. Whole numbers ending in 1, 3, 5, 7, and 9 are odd; those ending in 0, 2, 4, 6, and 8 are even.

Test Example

1. Is 36 odd or even?

   ○ odd

   ○ even

   ○ there's no way to tell

Think About the Answer

The number 36 has a 6 in the ones place. Six is an even number. This means that 36 must be an even number.

Now You Try It

2. Write an even number that is larger than 41.

_____

Check your answer on page 109.

KNOW THE SKILL: **Number Order
(Before, After, Between)**

Having a sense of number order means that when you see a number, you can tell what numbers come before and after it. On a test, you may see a list of numbers with blank spaces or missing numbers. Your job will be to fill in the missing numbers.

Test Example

1 What are the missing numbers that belong in the blank spaces?

34, 35, _____, _____, 38, _____

- ○ 36, 38, and 40
- ○ 36, 37, and 39
- ○ 36, 37, and 38

Think About the Answer

The numbers 36 and 37 belong in the spaces after 35. The number 39 belongs in the space after 38. The correct answer is the second one: 36, 37, and 39.

Now You Try It

2 Write the number that comes after 78.

_____

Check your answer on page 109.

Advantage Test Prep Grade 2 © 2004 Creative Teaching Press

KNOW THE SKILL: **Skip Counting by 2, 5, and 10**

Skip counting is a way to count groups of things instead of counting them one at a time. Use patterns for skip counting. For example, when you start with 0 and count by 5's, the numbers take turns ending in 0 and 5.

Test Example

1 Skip count by 5's to fill in the missing numbers.

5, 10, 15, ___, ___, ___, ___, ___, ___, 50

○ 25, 35, 45, 55, 65, 75

○ 16, 17, 18, 19, 20, 21

○ 20, 25, 30, 35, 40, 45

Think About the Answer

The third answer (20, 25, 30, 35, 40, 45) is correct.

Now You Try It

2 Skip count by 2's to complete this counting line.

2, _____, _____, _____, _____, _____, _____, _____, _____, 20

Check your answer on page 109.

KNOW THE SKILL: **Greater Than and Less Than**

We use the symbols > and < to compare numbers. The symbol > means *greater than*. The symbol < means *less than*. You already know the symbol = , which means *equal to*.

Test Example

1 Choose the symbol that belongs inside the circle to make this number sentence true.

37 ◯ 45

◯ >

◯ <

◯ =

Think About the Answer

The second choice (<) is the correct answer. The number 37 is smaller, or less than, 45. The way to read this expression is, "37 is less than 45."

Now You Try It

2 Write the symbol inside the circle to make this number sentence true.

91 ◯ 86

Check your answer on page 109.

Math

KNOW THE SKILL: **Ordinal Numbers**

Here are some different ways you can show number order for the numbers 1–10.

1	2	3	4	5	6	7	8	9	10
first	second	third	fourth	fifth	sixth	seventh	eighth	ninth	tenth
1st	2nd	3rd	4th	5th	6th	7th	8th	9th	10th

Test Example

 Draw a circle around the seventh .

Think About the Answer

To find the seventh apple, begin on the left and count to seven. The apple you touch last is the seventh. That is the one you should circle.

Now You Try It

 Draw a line through the ninth .

Check your answer on page 109.

KNOW THE SKILL: **Solve for a Missing Number**

When you know the sum and one of the addends in an addition problem, you can figure out the other addend. You can also find the one missing number in a subtraction equation if the others are known.

Test Example

1. What number belongs in the ☐ in the number sentence below?

    $6 +$ ☐ $= 11$

    ○ 5

    ○ 7

    ○ 6

Think About the Answer

This is an addition problem with a missing addend. You can read it this way: "Six plus what number will add up to 11." When adding, you can count up to get to the sum. By counting (7, 8, 9, 10, 11) we can see that it takes 5 numbers to go from 6 to 11. The correct answer is 5.

Now You Try It

2. What number belongs in the ☐ in the number sentence below?

    $15 -$ ☐ $= 9$

    ○ 24

    ○ 5

    ○ 6

Check your answer on page 109.

KNOW THE SKILL: **Fact Families**

Here is an example of a fact family using the numbers 2, 4, and 6:

Addition	Subtraction
4 + 2 = 6	6 − 2 = 4
2 + 4 = 6	6 − 4 = 2

Test Example

 1 Find the missing number in the fact family.

$3 + 4 = 7$ $\qquad$ $7 - 3 = 4$

$4 + 3 = 7$ $\qquad$ $\square - 4 = 3$

○ 7

○ 3

○ 4

Think About the Answer

This is a subtraction problem. We know the numbers in the fact family are 7, 3, and 4. The $\square$ is at the beginning of the sentence. That means that it should contain the largest number. The correct answer is 7.

Now You Try It

 2 Make a fact family for the numbers 5, 7, and 12.

_____ + _____ = _____ $\qquad$ _____ − _____ = _____

_____ + _____ = _____ $\qquad$ _____ − _____ = _____

Check your answer on page 109.

KNOW THE SKILL: **Counting Money**

You should be able to recognize the fronts and backs of pennies, nickels, dimes, quarters, half-dollars, and dollar bills when you see pictures of them. You also need to know their values. Skip counting can help you count money quickly.

Test Example

1 What is the total value of this money?

- ○ $1.68
- ○ 65 cents
- ○ $1.63

Think About the Answer

The second answer cannot be true because the money includes a dollar bill. The total must be over a dollar. The total of the coins is 68 cents. The first choice ($1.68) is correct.

Now You Try It

2 What is the value of this money? _____

Check your answer on page 109.

Advantage Test Prep Grade 2 © 2004 Creative Teaching Press

KNOW THE SKILL: **Telling Time**

You should be able to read the time on two different kinds of time pieces—clocks or watches with hands, and digital clocks with just numbers.

Test Example

 1 What time does this clock show?

- ○ 5:20
- ○ 4:25
- ○ 4:00

Think About the Answer

The hour hand is past the 4 but not yet to the 5. This means it is past 4:00. The minute hand is pointing to the 5. If you start at the 12 at the top of the clock and count by 5's (5, 10, 15, 20, 25), you know to add 25 minutes to 4:00. The time is 4:25.

Now You Try It

 2 What time does this clock show?

_____

Check your answer on page 109.

KNOW THE SKILL: **Measurement**

You may be asked to estimate or measure things in inches or feet and centimeters or meters.

Test Example

1 How long is this paper clip?

○ 4 inches

○ 1 inch

○ 2 inches

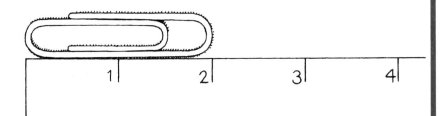

Think About the Answer

The ruler shows that the paper clip is exactly 2 inches long.

Now You Try It

2 How many centimeters is this pencil?

_____ centimeters

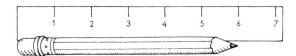

Check your answer on page 109.

KNOW THE SKILL: **Estimating**

When you estimate, you come close to the answer without counting or without adding or subtracting numbers on paper.

Test Example

1 Estimate the sum of 19 + 62.

- ○ about 70
- ○ about 80
- ○ about 90

Think About the Answer

The number 19 is close to 20. The number 62 is close to 60. You can quickly add 60 and 20 in your head. The second choice (about 80) is correct.

Now You Try It

2 Estimate the sum of 22 + 51.

about _____

Check your answer on page 109.

KNOW THE SKILL: **Addition with 2-Digit Numbers**

When adding 2-digit numbers, begin with the numerals in the ones place first. Add those two numerals together and record their sum in the ones place. If this sum is greater than 9, you may regroup and add the ten to the tens column before you begin to add it up.

Test Example

1 Solve this problem: 38 + 46 = ☐

- ○ 84
- ○ 73
- ○ 62

Think About the Answer

Adding the numbers in the way described above produces an answer like this:

$$\begin{array}{r} 1 \\ 38 \\ +46 \\ \hline 84 \end{array}$$

Now You Try It

2 Solve this problem: 19 + 33 = ☐

_____

Check your answer on page 109.

Advantage Test Prep Grade 2 © 2004 Creative Teaching Press

KNOW THE SKILL: **Subtraction with 2-Digit Numbers**

Subtraction with 2-digit numbers is similar to addition. One difference is that if the number in the ones place is lower for the top number than it is for the bottom, you will regroup one of the tens and bring it to the ones column.

Test Example

1 Solve this problem: 44 – 29 = ☐

　　　○ 24

　　　○ 26

　　　○ 15

Think about the Answer

Subtracting the numbers in the way described above produces an answer like this:

$$
\begin{array}{r}
3\ 1 \\
\cancel{44} \\
-\ 29 \\
\hline
15
\end{array}
$$

Now You Try It

2 Solve this problem: 41 – 24 = ☐

_____

Check your answer on page 109.

KNOW THE SKILL: **Fractions**

Fractions show parts of whole numbers. In a fraction like $\frac{1}{2}$, the top number is called the **numerator.** It tells you how many pieces of the fraction there are. The bottom number is called the **denominator.** It tells how many pieces the number has been cut into.

Test Example

1 What fraction of this bar is shaded?

○ $\frac{2}{5}$

○ $\frac{1}{5}$

○ $\frac{2}{3}$

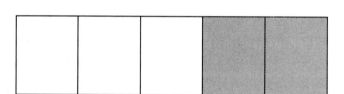

Think About the Answer

There are two pieces that are shaded. This means the numerator is 2. There are 5 pieces altogether. This means the denominator is 5. The correct answer is $\frac{2}{5}$.

Now You Try It

2 What fraction of this figure is shaded?

_____

Check your answer on page 109.

KNOW THE SKILL: Identifying Shapes

You should be familiar with common shapes such as circles, squares, rectangles, and triangles. You should also be able to identify the number of sides of 5-, 6-, 7-, and 8-sided figures.

Test Example

1 How many sides does this hexagon have?

○ 5

○ 4

○ 6

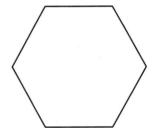

Think About the Answer

Sometimes the name of a figure can tell you how many sides it has. For example, *tri* means *three* and a triangle has 3 sides. The word beginning *hex* means *six*. The answer is 6.

Now You Try It

2 How many sides does this octagon have?

_____

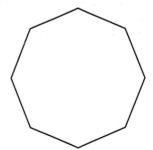

Check your answer on page 109.

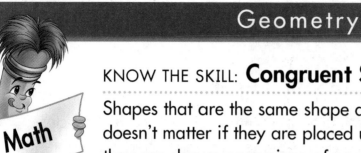

KNOW THE SKILL: **Congruent Shapes**

Shapes that are the same shape and size are **congruent.** It doesn't matter if they are placed upside down or sideways. If they are drawn on a piece of paper and cut out, they will fit exactly one over the other.

Test Example

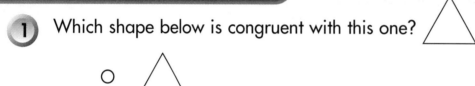

1. Which shape below is congruent with this one?

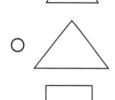

Think About the Answer

The third shape is a square, so it can't be congruent with a triangle. The second shape is a triangle, but it is not the same shape; it has two longer sides. The first shape is the same size and shape. It is the congruent one.

Now You Try It

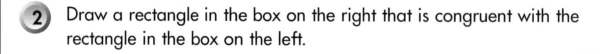

2. Draw a rectangle in the box on the right that is congruent with the rectangle in the box on the left.

Check your answer on page 109.

KNOW THE SKILL: **Symmetry**

A figure is **symmetrical** if you can draw a line right through the middle of it, fold the sides together, and both halves match. Circles are symmetrical. Squares and heart shapes are symmetrical, too. A shape that is longer on one side but not on the other is not symmetrical.

Test Example

1 Is this figure symmetrical?

- ○ no
- ○ yes
- ○ no way to tell

Think About the Answer

The figure is not the same on both sides. There is no place that you could draw a line that would cut it exactly in half. The answer is *no*, it is not symmetrical.

Now You Try It

2 Draw a symmetrical figure in the space below.

Check your answer on page 109.

Patterns and Relationships

KNOW THE SKILL: **Finding Patterns**

Some tests will ask you to find a pattern in a string of numbers, letters, or shapes. You will have to predict what would come next if the string were continued. It is a skill that involves finding or making up rules to fit what you are seeing.

Test Example

1 What would come next in this pattern?

A, A, B, B, C, C, ____, ____

- ○ A, B
- ○ D, E
- ○ D, D

Think About the Answer

The pattern in this string is double letters, moving through the alphabet. The correct answer is D, D.

Now You Try It

2 Continue the next three numbers of this pattern. Then tell what the rule is.

1, 3, 5, ____, ____, ____

_____ The rule is _____.

Check your answer on page 109.

Advantage Test Prep Grade 2 © 2004 Creative Teaching Press

Patterns and Relationships

KNOW THE SKILL: **Function Boxes**

The numbers in a function box have a relationship. In this example, the numbers in the Out column are 5 greater than the numbers in the In column. You would express this rule as +5.

In	Out
3	8
5	10
1	6

Test Example

1. What is the rule for this function box?

   ○ +4

   ○ −4

   ○ +1

In	Out
9	5
10	6
5	1

Think About the Answer

The rule is that the numbers in the Out column are 4 less than the numbers in the In column. The correct answer is −4.

Now You Try It

2. Complete this function box, which has a rule of +3.

In	Out
4	
6	9
2	

Check your answer on page 109.

Graphing

KNOW THE SKILL: **Showing Data**

Data is number information. If you ask 20 people what their favorite flavor of ice cream is, your results might look like this:

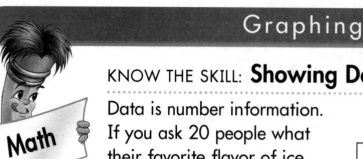

Our Class's
Favorite Kinds of Ice Cream

Chocolate	🍦🍦🍦🍦🍦🍦
Vanilla	🍦🍦🍦🍦🍦
Strawberry	🍦🍦
Other Kinds	🍦🍦🍦🍦🍦🍦🍦

Key: 🍦 = 1 person

Test Example

1 How many people liked strawberry ice cream best?

○ 6

○ 2

○ 20

Think About the Answer

Look for the line that has the word *Strawberry*. Count the number of marks on that line. The correct answer is 2.

Now You Try It

2 How many people liked "Other Kinds" of ice cream the best?

_____

Check your answer on page 109.

Advantage Test Prep Grade 2 © 2004 Creative Teaching Press

Problem Solving

KNOW THE SKILL: **Making a Plan**

When solving word problems, look for these key words:
altogether *means* add up numbers
more *means* add a number
less or fewer *means* subtract a number
take away *means* subtract a number
difference *means* compare numbers by subtracting

Test Example

1. What is this story problem asking you to do?

   Alma had 4 stickers. Her friend Zoe gave her 6 <u>more</u>. How many did Alma have <u>altogether</u>?

   ○ add 6 stickers

   ○ take away 4 stickers

   ○ add 4 stickers

Think About the Answer

The problem says that Alma already had 4 stickers. She needs to add Zoe's 6 stickers. The first choice (add 6 stickers) is correct.

Now You Try It

2. What is this story problem asking you to do?

   12 birds were on a wire. A dog scared some away and then there were 8 left. How many were scared away?

   ○ add 12

   ○ subtract 8

   ○ add 8

Check your answer on page 109.

KNOW THE SKILL: **Showing Your Work**

An important part of solving a word problem is being able to show how you did it. This can be done using pictures, words, numbers, and number sentences.

Test Example

1 Which math sentence best matches this picture?

○ $14 + 3 = 17$

○ $11 + 3 = 14$

○ $11 - 3 = 8$

Think About the Answer

The picture shows 11 apples. Three of the apples are crossed out. The sentence $11 - 3 = 8$ matches it the best.

Now You Try It

2 Write a math sentence to match this picture.

_____

Check your answer on page 109.

Practice Test Introduction

The rest of this book is a practice test. It's a lot like a standardized test students might take in school. It includes all of the skills students studied in this book. The questions in the test are similar to the ones students already practiced in previous pages.

The test is divided into the same sections as the earlier parts of the book. There are sections on reading, writing, language arts, and math. Here are some tips for students to keep in mind during the practice test:

- The test is meant to be a challenge. In your work in school and with this book, you have learned a lot. Enjoy the challenge of testing your skills.

- Make sure you understand all the directions before you start a section. Ask an adult if you have any questions about the directions.

- When you take the practice test, there is no time limit. Still, plan to work at a steady pace as a practice for test taking in school.

- Try to complete each section in one session. You will see a stop sign at the end of the section when you are done.

- If you don't know an answer, you can leave it blank and come back to it later.

- After you finish each section, you can check your answers in the back of the book, beginning on page 110.

Garnet's Promise

Garnet was a young eaglet that lived near the Columbia River.

She was a proud bird. She had great scooping wings. When she glided, her strong wings stretched wide. Her eyes were sharp. From high in the sky she could see ants on the ground.

Fish were afraid of her. She would swoop down and gobble them up before they could see her.

More than anything, Garnet wanted to find her family. When she first learned to fly, she had gone out hunting and gotten lost. Now she was alone. She could take care of herself in the forest, but she didn't want to be a young bird on her own.

One day, she dove into the river to catch a salmon. His name was Tim. Before she could grab him, he called out to her.

"Wait, please. I have something to tell you!" Tim said.

GO

Advantage Test Prep Grade 2 © 2004 Creative Teaching Press

A talking fish! Garnet was shocked. She pulled out of her dive and did a wide turn around the river. Then she flew back to the fish and hovered in the air above the river.

"I know where your family is," Tim said.

"How?" Garnet squawked.

"Another fish told me. We all know what goes on around here," Tim said.

"Please tell me where they are," Garnet pleaded.

"OK," Tim said, "but you have to make me a promise."

"Sure, anything," Garnet said. "I just want to get home."

"Tell the birds not to gobble us all up. There are plants they can eat too, you know."

Garnet promised. When Garnet got home, she began to talk to the mice and fish and other smaller creatures. From that day on, she learned to be a better bird.

1 What happened in this story?

○ A mouse and an eagle have a fight.

○ A salmon gets lost in a river.

○ An eagle learns a lesson.

2 Which is an *eaglet*?

○   ○   ○

3 The root word of *eaglet* is _____.

4 Choose the phrase that correctly completes the sentence.

Garnet was flying over the river _____.

○ to cool off

○ to catch fish

○ to find her family

5 Does Garnet have sharp eyes? Explain how you know.

_____

6 How did the fish know that Garnet was lost?

○ Another fish told him.

○ It was in the newspaper.

○ He heard it on the radio.

7 Which happened FIRST in the story?

○ Garnet flew over the river.

○ A baby eaglet got lost.

○ She promised not to hurt Tim.

8 Which picture shows how Garnet got lost?

○   ○   ○

9 What did Tim want to tell Garnet?

_____

_____

10 What was the name of the river near where Garnet lived?

○ Red River   ○ Columbia River   ○ Mississippi River

11 Would you be afraid of Garnet if you were a fish? Explain.

_____

_____

12 Choose the phrase that correctly completes the sentence.

Most of all, Garnet wanted to _____.

○ fly   ○ make friends   ○ find her way home

GO ➤

Read the passage and look at the diagram. Then answer questions 13 through 22.

How Your Body Works

Each moment your body is working. You can feel this, but you don't have to think to make it happen.

Your breathing takes oxygen (OX - a - jin) from the air. Every part of your body needs oxygen. It will not stay healthy if it does not get new oxygen all the time. That is why we are always taking in breaths or letting them out. It never stops. The oxygen goes from the lungs into your blood.

Blood is carried throughout your body by tiny tubes called veins and arteries. The heart is a pump that pushes the blood through these tiny tubes.

The heart sends the blood with fresh oxygen everywhere it needs to go. The heart also takes away the old blood that needs new oxygen from the lungs.

When you relax and breathe deeply, you give your body extra oxygen to help it be healthy. Play and exercise help you get stronger, take in more oxygen, and move your blood. They are healthy ways to spend your time.

Advantage Test Prep Grade 2 © 2004 Creative Teaching Press

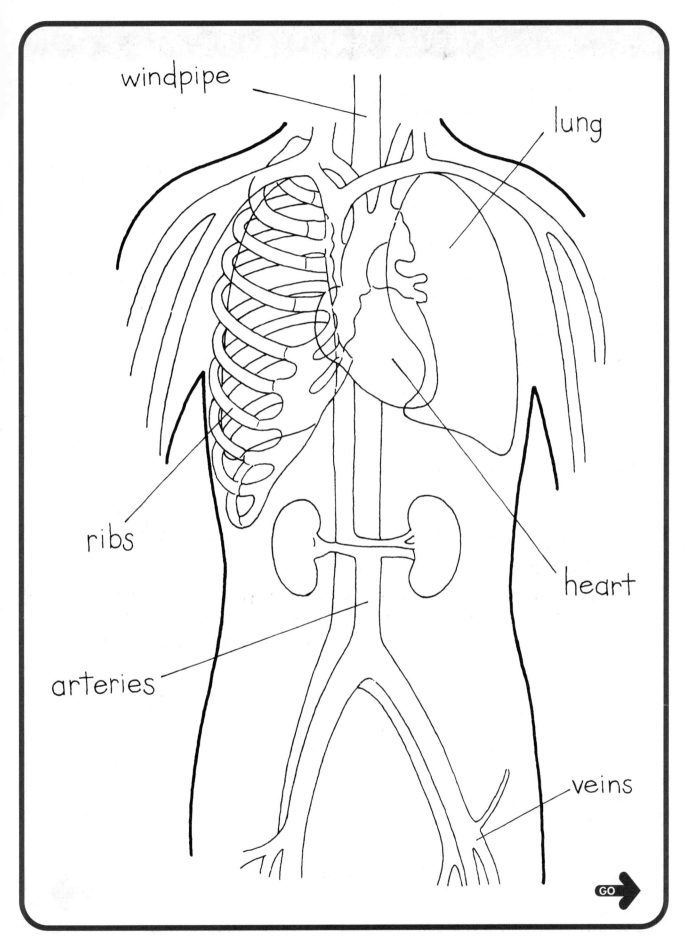

windpipe

lung

ribs

heart

arteries

veins

GO

13 What does your body use oxygen for?

_____

14 What pumps your blood through your body?

○ muscles   ○ lungs   ○ heart

15 What is another good title for this reading passage?

○ Heart, Lungs, and Oxygen

○ Exercise

○ Your Blood

16 Where does blood pick up oxygen? Circle the word on the diagram.

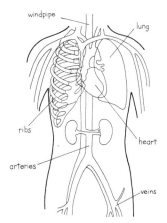

17 What is something that veins and arteries are like?

   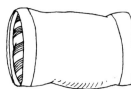   

○ a straw   ○ a pillow   ○ a balloon

Advantage Test Prep Grade 2 © 2004 Creative Teaching Press

18 Choose the phrase that correctly completes the sentence.

Our bodies need to work so hard because _____.

- ○ breathing takes strong muscles
- ○ oxygen is needed all the time
- ○ we need to think hard

19 Look at the diagram on page 85. Where is the heart?

- ○ inside the left lung
- ○ there is no heart in this diagram
- ○ between the two lungs

20 Which protects the lungs?

- ○ rib cage   ○ lungs   ○ the heart

21 What have you learned about keeping your body healthy?

_____

_____

22 What are some main ideas from this selection?

_____

_____

_____

STOP

Practice Test: Writing

Read the writing prompt and the writer's checklist. Then plan your writing.

Writing Prompt

Take a story you know from books you read or listened to in school. Make up a new adventure with the characters from this book. If you want, you can also put yourself in the story as a character.

Writer's Checklist

Check to make sure that you think about each of these points when you write your story:

- ☐ My story takes characters from a book I know.
- ☐ I made up and described new adventures for these characters.
- ☐ I made sure to use details to show what the adventure was like.
- ☐ My story has an introduction, a middle, and an end that tells what happened in the adventure.
- ☐ I have spelled second-grade spelling words right.
- ☐ Names and beginnings of sentences start with a capital letter.
- ☐ My sentences end with a period (.), a question mark (?), or an exclamation point (!).

Advantage Test Prep Grade 2 © 2004 Creative Teaching Press

Plan Your Writing

Use this space to plan your writing.

Sketch

Story Planner

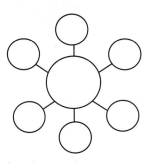

Mind Map

GO ➤

Write Your First Draft

Use all the skills you have learned to write a first draft.

_____

_____

_____

_____

_____

_____

_____

_____

_____

_____

_____

_____

_____

GO ➡

Advantage Test Prep Grade 2 © 2004 Creative Teaching Press

GO ➡

Write Your Final Draft

Now it's time to write your final draft. Use the writer's checklist on page 88 to help give you ideas for how to make your writing better.

_____

_____

_____

_____

_____

_____

_____

_____

_____

_____

_____

_____

GO →

Advantage Test Prep Grade 2 © 2004 Creative Teaching Press

Give Yourself a Score

Go back to the writing rubric on page 31. Give yourself a score from 4 to 0 for each category. Then ask someone else to score your writing so you will have two different sets of scores.

How I Scored It

Ideas	Organization	Sentence Structure	Spelling, Punctuation, and Grammar
_____	_____	_____	_____

How Someone Else Scored It

Ideas	Organization	Sentence Structure	Spelling, Punctuation, and Grammar
_____	_____	_____	_____

23 Which is a sentence?

    ○ give the ball to Joe

    ○ the ball to Mr. Gomez.

    ○ Give the ball to me.

24 Which is a sentence?

    ○ I don't.

    ○ Maybe 2:30.

    ○ It is hot.

25 Write the correct end mark at the end of the sentence.

Will you go with me ____

26 Which word does NOT need to start with a capital letter?

  ○ David   ○ Tree   ○ California

27 Write the words that make up the contraction **I'm.**

_____ + _____

28 Choose the date that correctly completes the sentence.

My little sister was born on _____.

○ May, 29 2003

○ May, 29, 2003

○ May 29, 2003

29 Rewrite the sentence with commas in the correct place.

I have a knife fork and spoon.

_____

30 Which is the noun?

Please give me the basketball.

○ give

○ basketball

○ please

31 Which of these is NOT a noun?

○ an action

○ a person

○ a thing

32 Write a verb on the line to complete the sentence.

Our dog likes to _____ other animals.

33 Which is a verb?

○ hair

○ Sally

○ think

34 Write a sentence that is about something happening now.

_____

_____

35 Which sentence is about something that already happened?

○ I played tag with Gina.

○ I will play tag with Gina.

○ He plays tag with Gina.

36 Another word for *big* is _____.

○ loud

○ strange

○ huge

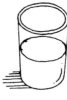

37 Look at the picture. The glass is empty.

Which picture shows the OPPOSITE of empty?

○   ○   ○

38 Which word best completes this sentence?

The soup was as hot as _____.

- ○ a box
- ○ a book
- ○ a fire

39 Which word best completes this sentence?

You can borrow my baseball _____ not my basketball.

- ○ and
- ○ or
- ○ but

40 Which word should replace the underlined words?

Our class was <u>more loud</u> than yours.

- ○ loud
- ○ loudest
- ○ louder

41 Which word belongs in the blank space?

He used to <u>plays</u> trumpet in the school band.

- ○ play
- ○ playing
- ○ played

42 Add two of these words together to make a compound word:
room, tape, bear, class.

_____ + _____ = _____

STOP

43 How many blocks are here?

○ 27

○ 35

○ 19

44 Which of these is an odd number?

○ 38

○ 15

○ 22

45 Which of these is an even number?

○ 47

○ 6

○ 65

For questions 46–48, choose the symbol that belongs inside the circle to make each number sentence true.

46 75 ◯ 34

○ >   ○ <   ○ =

47 38 ◯ 11

○ >   ○ <   ○ =

48 81 ◯ 81

○ >   ○ <   ○ =

Advantage Test Prep Grade 2 © 2004 Creative Teaching Press

49 What are the missing numbers that belong in the blank spaces?

23, 24, ____, ____, 27, ____

○ 25, 26, and 29

○ 25, 26, and 27

○ 25, 26, and 28

50 Write the number that comes **before** 48.

_____

51 Write the number that comes **between** 62 and 64.

_____

For questions 52–54, fill in the missing numbers to complete the pattern.

52

20	30		50			

53

25	30	35				

54

12	14			20		

GO →

55 Draw a circle around the fifth ⚑.

⚑ ⚑ ⚑ ⚑ ⚑ ⚑ ⚑

56 Draw a line through the 9th letter in this line of letters.

w b r t s u q x m e a z

For questions 57–59, choose the number that belongs in each ☐ in the number sentences below.

57 $4 + \boxed{} = 15$

○ 7

○ 11

○ 19

58 $\boxed{} + 8 = 17$

○ 9

○ 25

○ 8

59 $9 + \boxed{} = 12$

○ 12

○ 21

○ 3

60 Write the missing number in the ☐ in the fact family.

$5 + 9 = 14$ $14 - 9 = 5$

$9 + 5 = 14$ $\boxed{} - 5 = 9$

GO →

61 Make a fact family for the numbers 3, 8, and 11

_____ + _____ = _____   _____ − _____ = _____

_____ + _____ = _____   _____ − _____ = _____

62 What is the total value of this money?

○ 97 cents

○ 92 cents

○ 67 cents

63 What is the total value of this money?

○ 58 cents

○ 63 cents

○ 78 cents

64 What time does this clock show?

○ 4:03

○ 3:25

○ 4:15

65 What time does this clock show?

○ 10:35

○ 10:45

○ 9:35

66 What time does this clock show?

_____

67 How wide is this can?

- ○ 2 inches
- ○ 3 feet
- ○ 3 inches

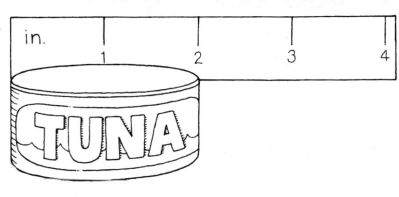

68 How long is this nail?

- ○ 4 inches
- ○ 3 feet
- ○ 3 inches

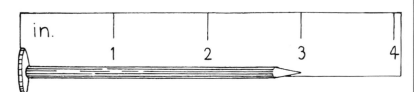

69 How long is this pushpin?

- ○ 1 centimeter
- ○ 1 foot
- ○ 2 inches

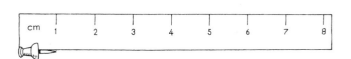

70 Estimate the sum of 11 + 37.

- ○ about 60
- ○ about 40
- ○ about 50

71 If there are about 20 dots in each group, how many dots do you think there are without counting them?

- ○ about 60
- ○ about 50
- ○ about 40

72 Estimate the difference of 62 − 30.

- ○ about 30
- ○ about 20
- ○ about 40

Advantage Test Prep Grade 2 © 2004 Creative Teaching Press

73 What is the sum?   20
  ○ 35   +15
  ○ 25   ──────
  ○ 40

74 What is the sum?   37
  ○ 62   +22
  ○ 59   ──────
  ○ 57

75 What is the sum?   56
  ○ 70   +24
  ○ 72   ──────
  ○ 80

76 What is the sum of 17 + 28?

  ○ 38   ○ 45   ○ 47

77 What is the difference?   56
  ○ 44   −20
  ○ 76   ──────
  ○ 36

78 What is the difference?   79
  ○ 90   −11
  ○ 78   ──────
  ○ 68

79 What is the difference?

$$\begin{array}{r} 68 \\ -29 \\ \hline \end{array}$$

- ○ 41
- ○ 40
- ○ 39

80 70 − 19 = ?

- ○ 51
- ○ 61
- ○ 89

81 What fraction of this figure is shaded?

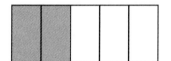

- ○ $\frac{2}{5}$
- ○ $\frac{2}{7}$
- ○ $\frac{3}{5}$

82 What fraction of the pie is shaded?

- ○ $\frac{1}{3}$
- ○ $\frac{4}{5}$
- ○ $\frac{1}{6}$

83 What is the name of this shape?

- ○ triangle
- ○ rectangle
- ○ trapezoid

84 How many sides does this pentagon have?

- ○ 6
- ○ 5
- ○ 4

85 Are these shapes congruent?

    ○ There's no way to tell.

    ○ No, they have different shapes.

    ○ Yes, they are the same.

86 Are these shapes congruent?

    ○ No, because they are different shapes.

    ○ Yes, because they are the same shape.

    ○ No, because they are different sizes.

87 Draw a line of symmetry on this triangle that would divide it into two equal parts.

88 Draw a figure that is symmetrical inside this box. Draw a line through the figure that divides it in half.

89 What would come next in this pattern?

A, B, B, C, C, C, ____, ____, ____, ____

    ○ D, D, D, D

    ○ D, E, F, G

    ○ D, D, E, E

90 What would come next in this pattern?

✔, ✘, ✘, ✔, ✘, ✘, ____, ____, ____

    ○ ✔, ✘, ✘

    ○ ✘, ✔, ✘

    ○ ✘, ✘, ✔

Use this function box to answer questions 91 and 92.

In	Out
10	3
12	5
9	2

91 What is the rule for this function box?

○ +7

○ +5

○ −7

92 If 17 were in the In box, what would be in the Out box?

○ 24   ○ 7   ○ 10

Use this chart to answer questions 93 and 94.

Eye Color in Our Class	
Brown	x x x x x x x x x x
Green	x x x x
Blue	x x x x x
Hazel	x x x

93 How many students have green eyes?

○ 3

○ 4

○ 5

94 How many students took part in the survey?

○ 22   ○ 12   ○ 20

95 What is this story problem asking you to do?

Nicky gave Chris 16 gumballs. Bill gave Chris 8 more. How many gumballs did Chris have altogether?

○ add 8 and 8

○ take away 8 from 16

○ add 16 and 8

Advantage Test Prep Grade 2 © 2004 Creative Teaching Press

Answer Key

Page 8
The answer is *food*. Minerals are something that gets taken in from the soil and helps the plant grow.

Page 9
The answer is *frozen*. This is the word that best describes an igloo. It is not *unfrozen* or a *freezer*.

Page 10
The answer is the last picture, the bean with a root sprouting from it. The soil is moist, so it would make the bean sprout. The growing plants could not have happened until the roots started.

Page 11
After is the word that tells time order.

Page 12
The correct answer is *light*. The passage talks about how plants use light. It talks about how seeds grow and mentions the sun, but it talks about more than those subjects.

Page 14
The correct answer is *when Joey's cards were missing*. This story mentions Ms. Willis' math group, but it is not about the math group. There is nothing about playing hockey in the story.

Page 15
Ms. Willis had picked up Joey's notebook on Ms. Perez' desk and walked away with it, thinking it was hers.

Page 16
The correct answer is *They looked alike*. The story doesn't say that Ms. Willis needed glasses. Also, teachers are not usually careless.

Page 17
The correct answer is *the notebook had hockey cards*. This is the only thing that was different about Joey's notebook.

Page 19
Answers will vary. Here is one possible answer: "What does the frog look like?"

Page 20
The correct answer is *the frog's coat*. The color of the water and the leaves are not mentioned in the poem.

Page 21
The correct answer is *gentle*.

Page 22
The correct answer is *south*.

Page 23
According to the chart, the correct answer is *December*.

Page 24
Diagrams will vary but should include arms, legs, eyes, ears, and a nose.

Page 25
Answers will vary. Possible answers include: goats, pigs, and ducks.

Page 26
The correct answer is *ball:* b-a-l comes before b-a-t in the dictionary because *l* comes before *t*. *Ladder* starts with an *l,* so it would come after the other two words.

Page 27
Winning a prize would make someone happy. The definition says that *jovial* means *happy.* The other choices would not make someone happy.

Page 28
The correct answer is *Flying to the Moon & Other Poems.* This is clear from the title and from the description next to the listing. *Our Solar System* is a video and *Stars and Planets* is nonfiction.

Page 29
The correct answer is *A–B.*

Page 40
The correct answer is *kicked.*

Page 41
Sentences will vary. Here are possible answers:
Question: Will you come with me?
Statement: I will come with you.
Exclamation: That's just great!

Page 42
Answers will vary. Here is one possible answer:
We live in New York.

Page 43
he'll, let's, couldn't, you're, that's, I'm

Page 44
The flag of France is red, white, and blue.

Page 45
Laura, eggs, and *Mom* are the nouns.

Page 46
Made is the verb.

Page 47
Climbed does not belong because it is the only past tense verb. All the other verbs are present tense.

Page 48
Answers will vary. Here are some possible answers: tiny, beautiful, chilly, quick, friendly, start, finish, task, big.

Page 49
Answers will vary. Here are some possible answers: tiny, pretty, cold, dry, dim, hot, empty, sad, dirty.

Page 50
hot

Page 51
But or *and* will work in this sentence.

Page 52
slower

Page 53
rowing

Page 54
race + track

Page 56
There are 55 blocks.

Advantage Test Prep Grade 2 © 2004 Creative Teaching Press

Page 57
Any even number above 42 would be correct. Even numbers end with the numbers 0, 2, 4, 6, and 8.

Page 58
79

Page 59
4, 6, 8, 10, 12, 14, 16, 18

Page 60
91 > 86

Page 61

Page 62
6

Page 63
5 + 7 = 12; 7 + 5 = 12; 12 − 7 = 5;
12 − 5 = 7

Page 64
$2.41

Page 65
1:15

Page 66
6 centimeters

Page 67
about 70

Page 68
19 + 33 = 52

Page 69
41 − 24 = 17

Page 70
$\frac{3}{8}$

Page 71
8 sides

Page 72
Any rectangle that is 3 x 1 will be congruent.

Page 73
Figures will vary. Figures must be symmetrical to be correct.

Page 74
7, 9, 11; The rule is going up by 2.

Page 75

In	Out
4	**7**
6	9
2	**5**

Page 76
7

Page 77
subtract 8

Page 78
5 + 4 = 9

Practice Test Answer Key

1 In this story, an eagle learns a lesson.

2 An eaglet is a bird. The first picture of a bird is the correct answer.

3 eagle

4 to catch fish

5 Yes, she has great vision. The reader knows this because the author says Garnet can see ants on the ground when she flies.

6 Another fish told him.

7 A baby eaglet got lost.

8 Garnet got lost because she went flying by herself. The first picture of Garnet flying alone is the correct answer. The second picture is not correct because Garnet did not get lost because of a storm. The third picture is not correct because Garnet did not get lost because she talked to a fish.

9 Answers will vary. Here's one possible answer: Tim wanted to tell Garnet how she could find her family. He also wanted to tell her not to eat him.

10 Columbia River

11 Answers will vary. Here is one possible answer: I would be afraid of Garnet because she is big and fast. She can swoop down and pick things up.

12 find her way home

13 Answers will vary. Correct answers should include that the body uses oxygen to stay healthy.

14 heart

15 Heart, Lungs, and Oxygen

16 The word *lung* on the diagram should be circled.

17 a straw

18 oxygen is needed all the time

19 between the two lungs

20 rib cage

21 Answers will vary. Here is one possible answer: One idea is to relax and take deep breaths. This will help you get more oxygen. Another good thing to do is get lots of exercise.

22 Answers will vary. Here is one possible answer: Our bodies need oxygen. We take it in through our lungs. Oxygen gets into our blood and travels through the veins and arteries.

23 Give the ball to me.

Advantage Test Prep Grade 2 © 2004 Creative Teaching Press

24 It is hot.

25 ?

26 Tree

27 I + am

28 May 29, 2003

29 I have a knife, fork, and spoon.

30 basketball

31 an action

32 Answers will vary. Possible answers include *chase* and *play with*.

33 think

34 Answers will vary but must be present tense to be correct. Here's one possible answer: I am studying how to take tests

35 I played tag with Gina.

36 huge

37 The picture of the full glass is correct.

38 a fire

39 but

40 louder

41 play

42 class + room = classroom

43 27

44 15

45 6

46 >

47 >

48 =

49 25, 26, and 28

50 47

51 63

52 | 20 | 30 | **40** | 50 | **60** | **70** | **80** |

53 | 25 | 30 | 35 | **40** | **45** | **50** | **55** |

54 | 12 | 14 | **16** | **18** | 20 | **22** | 24 |

55

56 w b r t s u q x Ɐ e a z

57 11

58 9

59 3

60 14

61 3 + 8 = 11; 11 − 3 = 8;
8 + 3 = 11; 11 − 8 = 3

62 92 cents

63 78 cents

64 4:15

65 10:45

66 12:20

67 2 inches

68 3 inches

69 1 centimeter

70 about 50

71 about 40

72 about 30

73 35

74 59

75 80

76 45

77 36

78 68

79 39

80 51

81 $\frac{2}{5}$

82 $\frac{1}{6}$

83 triangle

84 5

85 Yes, they are the same.

86 No, because they are different sizes.

87

88 Answers will vary. To be correct, figures must be symmetrical and have a line dividing the figure in half.

89 D, D, D, D

90 ✔, ✘, ✘

91 −7

92 10

93 4

94 22

95 add 16 and 8